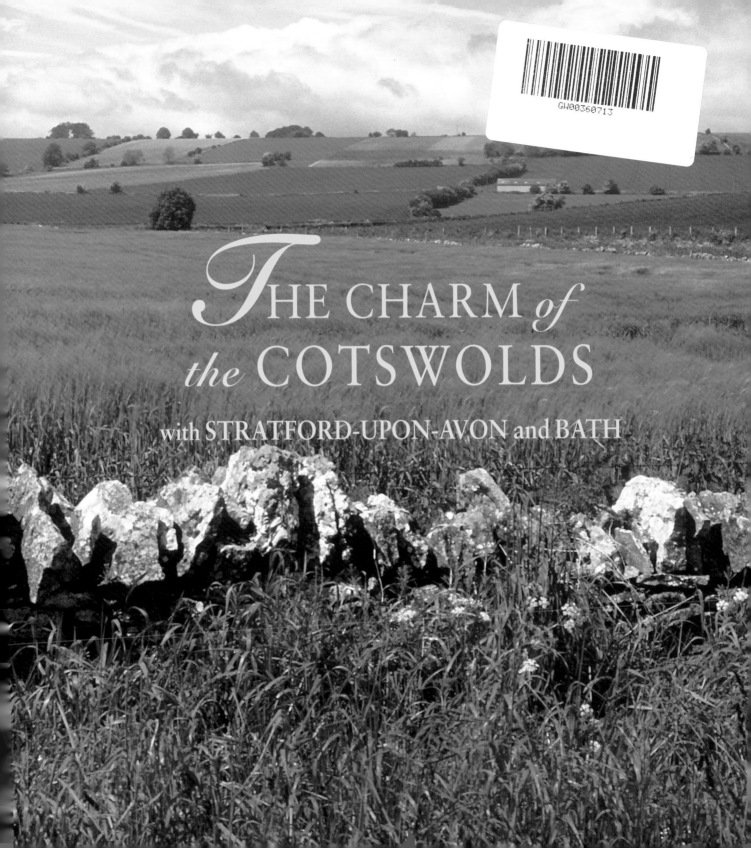

# THE CHARM of
# the COTSWOLDS

## with STRATFORD-UPON-AVON and BATH

# *S*LOW LANE SOUTH
## THE COTSWOLD WAY

The Cotswold Way winds slowly south, a quiet journey through distance and time, past neolithic burial mounds, ancient abbeys and castles, simple country cottages, stylish town houses – a parade of the nation's architecture from Roman to Regency and beyond. Inaugurated some twenty-five years ago by the Ramblers' Association and Gloucestershire County Council, the Way begins at Chipping Campden and ends, a hundred miles later, at the great abbey in Bath, that most elegant of cities. In between lies some of the finest, most unspoilt countryside in southern Britain, uncrowded, uncluttered – almost unnoticed.

**Heritage in trust**

The National Trust protects many Cotswold treasures, beautiful areas of countryside, Roman villas, ruined abbeys, even whole villages. In the far south the Cotswold Way passes one of the Trust's outstanding houses at Dyrham Park.

**Vineyard Row, Winchcombe**

As you might suspect, wine was once produced here, as was tobacco in the seventeenth century. Winchcombe, just twelve miles along the route of the Cotswold Way, was once the capital of Saxon Mercia.

**Dreaming spires**

The Way passes many examples of fine ecclesiastical architecture; a particularly graceful example *(right)* is at Painswick, almost half-way along the route.

**Cleeve Hill – the roof of the world**

At about 300 metres above sea level, Cleeve Hill *(main picture)* is the highest point along the Cotswold Way.

## Glorious view

Take a well-earned rest from your walk to contemplate the Vale of Evesham, seen here at Snowshill in Gloucestershire.

## Chipping Campden

Of all the Cotswold towns, Chipping Campden must rank as one of the most beautiful. Founded on the prosperity of the wool trade, its houses (*pictured right*) are characterised by undulating roofs and mullioned windows.

**Holy Trinity Church**

This Gothic church is where William Shakespeare was both christened and buried. The registry book recording his christening on 26 April 1564 is in the town's records office close to Shakespeare's birthplace. Shakespeare grew up as a firm believer in the Anglican faith and worshipped here regularly. His tomb, in front of the altar, is marked by a simple, engraved stone.

# $\mathcal{S}$HAKESPEARE'S TOWN – STRATFORD-UPON-AVON

Towards the end of the sixteenth century a talented and ambitious young playwright staged his first-ever play. *Henry VI, Part One* became a huge success. Suitably encouraged, William Shakespeare continued to write and Stratford's future was secured. Today this picturesque Warwickshire town, with its well-preserved Tudor half-timbered buildings, retains the face of Merrie England with many reminders of the nation's greatest literary genius. The River Avon, which meanders through the centre, passes not only the main theatres and the Holy Trinity Church, but is also flanked by some well-kept lawns, creating a green corridor through this most historic of places.

**Shakespeare's birthplace**

William Shakespeare, the third child of John and Mary Shakespeare, was born on or about 23 April 1564 in this relatively modest house in Henley Street. His father is thought to have been a glove merchant and city alderman. William later inherited the house.

## Horneby Cottage

This fifteenth-century cottage is next to Shakespeare's birthplace. Thomas Horneby was a blacksmith and neighbour of Shakespeare. It is now owned by the Birthplace Trust and is a souvenir shop.

## Anne Hathaway's Cottage

Situated just over a mile away from Stratford in the pretty village of Shottery is Anne Hathaway's cottage, the birthplace of the woman who was to become Shakespeare's wife. Anne was eight years older than Shakespeare and already pregnant when she married him in 1582.

### Museum of medieval medicine

Hall's Croft is a fine medieval house which was once the home of Shakespeare's elder daughter Susanna and her doctor-husband John Hall. The best view of the house is from the back.

### The dispensary in Hall's Croft

Kept the way it was in Tudor times, the dispensary is laid out as it would have been when Hall practised here.

## PORTRAIT OF THE BARD

Shakespeare left Stratford for London at around 1586 to seek fame and fortune. His plays, more than three dozen major works ranging from the great tragedies to sweeping historical drama and riotous comedy, all poured out in just over two decades. *Henry V, Much Ado About Nothing* and *Julius Caesar* were all completed in a single year. Indeed, Shakespeare was so prolific and diverse in his creative output that it was later doubted that he had written all the plays himself. He had started his theatrical career as an actor, often performing in his own plays; later he also became a theatre owner. Writing no more after 1612, he retired to Stratford a relatively wealthy man, to live out his remaining four years quietly amongst his family.

## The stage is set

The interior of the Swan Theatre with the stage in the centre of the auditorium has a definite flavour of the original Elizabethan theatres, which had developed out of the courtyards of coaching inns where plays had once been performed. The major works of Shakespeare are regularly staged at Stratford by the Royal Shakespeare Company.

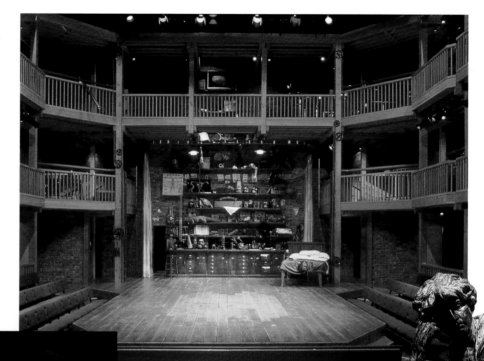

## Mary Arden's House

The family home of Shakespeare's mother, Mary Arden, can be found in Wilmcote, three miles to the north of Stratford. The house is a beautiful example of an Elizabethan half-timbered farmhouse, as Mary came from a family of wealthy landowners. It has an enormous dovecote, at one time home to a thousand doves.

## Alas poor Yorick

This statue of Hamlet is part of an extensive monument to the immortal bard by Lord Ronald Gower in the Bancroft Gardens on the banks of the river.

## Shakespeare live

This performance of *Julius Caesar* performed at the Royal Shakespeare Theatre by the Royal Shakespeare Company in 1995 was directed by Sir Peter Hall with Hugh Quarshie as Mark Antony and John Nettles as Marcus Brutus.

## Stratford's theatres

The Shakespeare Memorial Theatre first opened in Stratford in 1879 with a performance of *Much Ado About Nothing*. It was renamed the Royal Shakespeare Theatre in 1961 with a very young Peter Hall as artistic director of the embryonic Royal Shakespeare Company. In 1986 a new theatre opened adjacent to the Royal Shakespeare called the Swan (*pictured right*). It was named after the original theatre built in London in 1596, and is mainly used for works by Shakespeare's contemporaries. A third theatre in Stratford, The Other Place, is devoted to more modern productions.

## Curtain call

Shakespeare's memorial in Holy Trinity Church was erected shortly after his death, supposedly the result of a heavy drinking session with fellow playwright Ben Jonson. The epitaph reads, 'In judgement a Nestor, in wit a Socrates, in art a Virgil. The earth covers him, the people mourn him, Olympus has him.' Shakespeare's grave is also within the church; the inscription, 'Bleste y man y spares thes stones and curst be he y moves my bones', was reputedly devised by the bard prior to his death on 23 April 1616.

## Caught in the act

Just outside Stratford lies Charlecote Park, home of the Lucy family since 1247. The present house with its magnificent gatehouse was built in the mid-sixteenth century and subsequently visited by Elizabeth I. The River Avon flows through a park landscaped by 'Capability' Brown which supports a large herd of deer. Shakespeare is said to have been caught poaching by the then owner Sir Thomas Lucy, having 'by a misfortune common enough to young fellows, fallen into ill company'.

## HARVARD HOUSE AND THE GARRICK INN

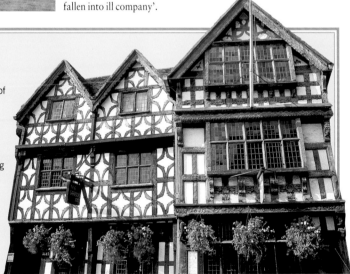

The ornately carved house bearing the flag-pole is Harvard House, formerly the home of John Harvard after whom the great American university takes its name. The property was presented to Harvard University in 1909. Harvard was a graduate of Emmanuel College, Cambridge, and emigrated to the New World in 1637 because of religious persecution. He died in Massachusetts a year later, barely thirty years old, bequeathing his library and half his estate to the 'shoale or colledge at Newetowne', later renamed Cambridge in honour of the large number of students who went to America from that university. Adjacent to Harvard House is the Garrick Inn. It takes its name from the actor-manager David Garrick who came to Stratford in 1769 to launch a Shakespearian festival, the first of its kind.

## Beautiful house, beautiful garden

The garden at Bourton House boasts splendid herbaceous borders, tinkling fountains, a topiary walk and a knot garden. Largely the creation of the present owners, they regularly add new features such as the raised pond in the top garden.

**Wondrous birds**

The raised pond at Bourton House provides the perfect setting for these serene and graceful sculptures.

# GREAT GARDENS OF THE NORTHERN COTSWOLDS

The route southwards from Stratford-upon-Avon to Chipping Campden passes seventeenth-century Hidcote Manor, which features one of England's most outstanding gardens in the delightful hamlet of Hidcote Bartrim. Created by the great horticulturist Major Lawrence Johnston early this century, Hidcote consists of a series of small gardens within a larger whole, each one in a different style, so that there is something of interest round every corner. Other wonderful gardens in the area include Kiftsgate, a highly imaginative garden in the same village as Hidcote; Bourton House at Bourton-on-the-Hill, which also has a fine tithe barn; and Sezincote, just outside Bourton, an extraordinarily exotic creation tucked away in the Cotswold Hills.

## Sezincote – Cotswold cultural shock

Beyond a long avenue of oak trees lies a house and garden that have more in common with a Moghul palace than an English country house. Sir Charles Cockerell originally financed Sezincote from a fortune made in the East India Company during the eighteenth century. Sir Cyril Kleinwort bought the estate in 1944 and the Paradise Garden was laid out by Lady Kleinwort on returning from India in 1965. The view of the house up the long canal brings to mind the Taj Mahal.

## Kiftsgate – a continuous calendar of colour

Dazzlingly bright lilies, huge hydrangeas, daffodils lining the drive in spring, Japanese maples glowing in autumn – there is always something to attract the visitor, whatever the time of year. Kiftsgate was first laid out in the 1920s, and although it is designed on a smaller scale than Hidcote, its relaxed atmosphere gives it a rather special appeal.

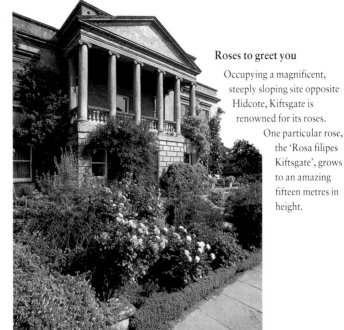

### Roses to greet you

Occupying a magnificent, steeply sloping site opposite Hidcote, Kiftsgate is renowned for its roses. One particular rose, the 'Rosa filipes Kiftsgate', grows to an amazing fifteen metres in height.

### The Pillar Garden at Hidcote

Johnston was a superb plantsman who had a wonderful knack of combining formality with the exuberance of a cottage garden. Imaginative yet highly disciplined, he excelled in profuse planting with strong colours and textures to create a highly personal style of garden.

### A stylish gazebo

The architectural features are an important aspect of Hidcote; the garden buildings, gateways and furniture are all worthy of note.

### 'Stow-on-the-Wold – where the wind blows cold'

The highest town in the Cotswolds was founded in the eleventh century astride the Fosse Way on a very exposed, windswept site from which the ground drops away on all sides. It quickly became a thriving market town, its prosperity being founded on wool, and in the seventeenth century as many as 20,000 sheep were sold at the Stow Fair. Today there is a biannual horse fair in the town, which was originally known as Edwinstowe or Stow St Edward, still reflected in the name of the church, school and Victorian hall in the centre of the fine market square.

# THE STAR ATTRACTIONS
## NORTH COTSWOLD TOWNS AND VILLAGES

Chipping Campden, Moreton-in-Marsh, Stow-on-the-Wold, Bourton-on-the-Water and Broadway – these five small towns are so popular with tourists in the summer months that they have come to be known as 'the famous five'. Nestling within the limestone hills, these impossibly picturesque places are best visited early in the morning or later in the day, when their streets become quieter and less crowded. The use of local limestone as a building material is a strongly unifying feature, giving the buildings a characteristic golden hue.

### Broadway

The best known of the Cotswold towns, Broadway is in the county of Hereford and Worcester and takes its name from a very wide high street, so constructed because it originally had two streams running through it. A brilliant collection of medieval, Tudor and Georgian architecture lines the main streets.

### Where three counties meet

Moreton-in-Marsh derives its name from march or boundary. The town straddles the Fosse Way at the boundaries of Warwickshire, Gloucestershire and Oxfordshire. Once it was an important staging post as reflected in the late-seventeenth- and early-eighteenth-century houses lining the High Street. A notable feature is the sixteenth-century Curfew Tower; its bell used to be rung nightly as a signal to the townsfolk to douse their fires.

## 'Venice of the Cotswolds'

The centre of Bourton-on-the-Water has the River Windrush flowing through wide, shady tree-lined lawns, its quiet waters crossed by numerous ornamental bridges, the oldest dating back to the mid- eighteenth century. In the High Street there is an ingenious model of the village, built of Cotswold stone on such a large scale that there is even a model of the model! Other attractions such as the motor museum, bird garden and perfumery make Bourton exceedingly popular with visitors.

## The sign of success

One of the most famous of the original Cotswold coaching inns, the Lygon Arms in Broadway is named after a general who fought at Waterloo and sold the building to his enterprising former butler who named it after his master, adopting for good measure the family coat-of-arms as the inn sign.

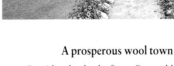

## Tribute to the mason's artistry

Almost every building in Chipping Campden is worth viewing. Be it manor house, church or cottage, each one is a worthy tribute to the mason's artistry.

## A prosperous wool town

Considered to be the finest Cotswold market town, Chipping Campden at the northern tip of the region derives its name from the Anglo-Saxon 'caepen', meaning market, and is the historic centre of the region's traditional wool trade. Wool produced enormous wealth which in turn created the town's rich vein of architecture, ranging from the Jacobean market hall to the Gothic brilliance of Grevel's House, named after a wealthy fourteenth-century merchant.

**Clapper bridges
in Lower Slaughter**

A shallow stream
glides through the
centre of the village,
crossed by a
number of simple
but beautifully
proportioned little
clapper bridges.

**Stanway – where thatch prevails**
Unusually, the roofs of the cottages are thatched in Stanway. Even the cricket pavilion is thatched; it was
presented by cricket fanatic Sir James Barrie, creator of *Peter Pan*. At the entrance to the village is an eye-
catching war memorial depicting St George slaying the dragon.

**India comes to the Cotswolds**
Samuel Pepys Cockerell created nearby Sezincote on
which the Prince Regent based the Brighton Pavilion.
It is thought that he also built this highly unusual
cottage at Lower Swell, which also takes its
inspiration from ancient Indian art.

# *L*ESSER-KNOWN
# NORTH COTSWOLD VILLAGES

Whilst 'the famous five' have the starring roles,
there are many other Cotswold villages that are
equally attractive yet often overlooked. Two such
villages are Stanton and Stanway, which straddle the
Cotswold Way close to Broadway. Many argue that
Stanton is the finest village in the Cotswolds, yet its
streets remain virtually deserted even in high summer.
Nearby, Snowshill, Guiting Power and Naunton enjoy a
similar situation, as do Upper and Lower Swell. Not far
from Bourton-on-the-Water the Slaughters also manage
to keep a low profile.

**Rush hour in Stanton**

Less than five miles from
busy Broadway, Stanton is
a much quieter village in a
superb situation. Its fine state
of preservation is due to the
efforts of Sir Philip Stott,
and it has much to offer the
visitor, including a medieval
wayside cross, Norman
church, the Jacobean Stanton
Court, a fifteenth-century
manor house, and many
Cotswold-stone cottages.

### Arlington Row, Bibury

With their steep, stone-tiled roofs and clutter of dormer windows, these former weavers' cottages are examples of vernacular architecture at its very best.

**Snowshill Manor**

This Tudor house, perched on the top of a hill overlooking the Vale of Evesham, was virtually derelict when purchased by Charles Paget Wade in 1919. He devoted most of the rest of his life to restoring it, presenting it to the National Trust in 1951.

# Historic Houses
## GREAT NORTH COTSWOLD RESIDENCES

Stanway House, the fascinating Jacobean mansion just south of Stanton, has been owned by only two families since it was built during the reign of James I. The last surviving member of the original family, Susan Tracy-Keck, whose father was killed in a duel in Hyde Park in 1767, married the eighth Earl of Wemyss. The Tracys were a colourful crowd, numbering among them a pirate, a heretic whose body was exhumed and burnt at the stake, and one of the knights who murdered Thomas à Becket in Canterbury Cathedral. Other superb houses nearby include the fifteenth-century Buckland Rectory which has a fine Great Hall, and Snowshill Manor in the village of the same name which is best known for its huge eclectic collections of Samurai armour, ancient bicycles, musical instruments and tools of the wool trade, originally assembled by the former owner, Charles Paget Wade.

**Wade's cottage**

The somewhat eccentric Wade chose not to live in Snowshill Manor but in an adjacent cottage which had a teak statue of St George mounted on the facade. He was an avid collector and scorned new-fangled devices such as electricity. Visitors included Virginia Woolf, Sir John Betjeman and Clough Williams-Ellis, among others. Wade loved playing amateur dramatics with his friends, dressing up in gorgeous costumes from his collection.

**Stanway**

In contrast to many other Cotswold residences Stanway has huge windows, the oriel window in the Great Hall being divided into sixty panels and almost reaching the eaves.

## A fine facade

Stanway House stands well back from the road in a large area of parkland dotted with oak trees. Its Renaissance facade is exceptionally fine.

## Grand entrance

The elaborate gateway to Stanway House is so stylish in appearance that it was once thought to be the work of Inigo Jones. In the grounds is a massive fourteenth-century tithe barn and a graveyard for dogs dating back to 1700.

## Eating together

The Great Hall at Stanway House is one of the last great halls to be built before owners and servants took to eating in separate rooms. Like the rest of the house, it has a pleasantly lived-in feeling rather than the atmosphere of a pristine museum. The present owner is the twelfth Earl of Wemyss and March, and the house is occupied by his son, Lord Neidpath.

### A beautiful setting

Not much of the Abbey's original complex survives, save for seventeen weather-worn cloister arches standing in peaceful surroundings. The Cotswold Way runs past the abbey entrance.

### To be a pilgrim

Today tourists have replaced pilgrims as a source of income to the abbey. Hailes is owned by the National Trust and administered by English Heritage.

### A romantic ruin

On the east side, leading into the Chapter House, is the heart of a Cistercian monastery, where the monks gathered each day to listen to a chapter from the rule of St Benedict, founder of Christian monasticism in western Europe.

### The word according to St Bernard

'It is good to be here. Here man more purely lives, less oft doth fall, more promptly rises, walks with stricter head, more safely rests, dies happier, is freed earlier from cleansing fires and gains withall a brighter glow.' This quotation is on the north wall of the cloister from the man who relaunched the Cistercian movement.

BONUM EST NOS HIC ESSE, QUIA HOMO VIVIT PURIUS, CADIT RARIUS, SURGIT VELOCIUS, INCEDIT CAUTIUS, QUIESCIT SECURIUS, MORITUR FELICIUS, PURGATUR CITIUS, PRÆMIATUR COPIOSIUS;
SAINT BERNARD.

# HAILES ABBEY 'IT IS GOOD TO BE HERE'

On a dark and stormy night in the early thirteenth century, Richard, Earl of Cornwall, brother of Henry III, was in danger of being consigned to a watery grave as his ship foundered during a great storm off the Scillies. He vowed that if spared he would build a monastery. His frantic prayer was duly answered and in 1246 Hailes Abbey was founded on a beautiful Cotswold site between Stanway and Winchcombe with a group of Cistercian monks drafted in from Beaulieu in Hampshire. When Richard's son gave the abbey a phial of blood, supposedly that of Christ, the abbey's place on the pilgrim trail was secure. All was well until Henry VIII declared the holy relic a fake and with somewhat insensitive timing closed the abbey on Christmas Eve 1539.

**Older than the Abbey**

Hailes parish church dates from the twelfth century. Its superb medieval wall paintings and stained glass windows have been carefully restored and depict both secular and ecclesiastical paintings. The Hailes Music Festival takes place each July at the church and other nearby venues and features classical music and jazz.

## DISSOLUTION OF THE MONASTERIES

Although in Henry VIII's reign there were almost 1,000 monasteries and nunneries containing some 17,000 men and women in Holy Orders, the monastic system had been in decline for some time, many communities being less than half full and very corrupt. More concerned with wealth than piety, the monasteries had become unpopular with both aristocracy and the middle classes. Henry astutely perceived that seizing the buildings and their estates would considerably enhance the royal purse without causing a public outcry. Thomas Cromwell carried out the king's wishes with ruthless efficiency and throughout the nation the great abbeys closed. Elsewhere in the region, Winchcombe, Cirencester, Malmesbury and Bath suffered the same fate.

## Catherine Parr's tomb

Shortly after Henry VIII died his sixth wife married her former lover, the powerful yet over-ambitious Sir Thomas Seymour, and came to live in his Cotswold stronghold. There was no happy ever after – Catherine died in childbirth only eighteen months after Henry, and Seymour was executed for treason. Catherine's tomb is in St Mary's Chapel in the grounds of Sudeley Castle.

## King Charles slept here

The king used this magnificent carved bed whilst campaigning in the Civil War. His impressive portrait by Van Dyck hangs in the North Hall. Sudeley was badly damaged in the war and remained in ruins for nearly 200 years until purchased and restored by the Dent family in 1837.

# DAYS OF GREATNESS AND GLORY

## SUDELEY CASTLE AND WINCHCOMBE

History's shadow lies heavy on this north-west corner of the Cotswolds. Three of Henry VIII's wives came to Sudeley Castle, Catherine Parr ending her days here. Following the defeat of the Armada, Queen Elizabeth held festivities for three days in the banqueting hall which was later ruined when the castle was attacked in the Civil War. Henry closed the monastery in nearby Winchcombe on the same day as Hailes Abbey was closed in 1539, and the walls of Winchcombe's parish church are riddled with Civil War bullet holes.

## Towers and turrets

Sudeley Castle, with its lake, towers and turrets, conveys images of white knights, dragons and damsels in distress. Set in magnificent grounds, its treasures include a lace coverlet by Anne Boleyn, made whilst awaiting execution, Catherine Parr's prayer book, and a glorious portrait of Elizabeth I in the south window.

### Dent's Terrace, Winchcombe

Next to the Plaisterers' Arms, this fine row of Victorian almshouses, the work of Sir Gilbert Scott, was endowed through the generosity of Emma Dent, the nineteenth-century owner of Sudeley.

### Making faces

St Peter's Church at Winchcombe is noted for its gargoyles – forty in all – a mixture of demons and caricatures of local fifteenth-century worthies.

### The parish church at Winchcombe

St Peter's Church is fifteenth-century Perpendicular architecture at its best, remaining virtually as it was when completed in 1468. The interior contains some magnificent treasures including the twelfth-century churchwarden's chest, an intricate altar cloth attributed to Catherine of Aragon during her stay at Sudeley, and the massive east window depicting St Peter trying to walk on water whilst Christ quells a storm.

**'The most beautiful village in England'**

This was Bibury as described by William Morris. The seventeenth-century Arlington Mill is now a folk museum and contains a fine room dedicated to Morris, while at the side of the mill is a trout farm.

# *T*ALK OF THE DEVIL
## BURIAL GROUNDS, BIBURY AND BURFORD

*T*ake the high ground south of Winchcombe for rugged country and panoramic views. This is an ancient land with neolithic burial grounds and the dramatic Devil's Chimney overlooking the Regency town of Cheltenham and beyond. Further east is the Cotswolds' finest medieval 'wool' church at Northleach on the Fosse Way, once tramped by Roman legions. Burford, the eastern gateway to the Cotswolds, is an elegant town situated in the Windrush Valley, while Bibury is a must for anyone interested in William Morris and the Pre-Raphaelites.

**The view from Belas Knap**

Belas Knap, a fine example of a neolithic long barrow, crowns a steep hill overlooking Winchcombe. Dating from 3000 BC, its name is derived from the Anglo-Saxon 'bel' (a beacon) and 'cnaepp' (a hill top).

**On a high – the Devil's Chimney**

Located two miles south of Cheltenham, where the Cotswold Way runs over Leckhampton Hill, stands the Devil's Chimney, theatrically poised on the edge of the cliff face. The Chimney is actually located in a huge quarry, originally dug to provide stone for the construction of nearby Cheltenham. This limestone outcrop is a dramatic remnant of those quarrying days.

## Burford, where the Cotswolds 'blow hot and cold'

Summer temperatures can reach the nineties but winter can bring an altogether different picture, as shown in this view of Burford's main street. The Tolsey or Court House was once a Tudor market house where the wealthy wool merchants gathered; it is now a museum housing the original charter and seals of the town and a splendid sixteenth-century mace.
Nell Gwynne's son by Charles II was created the Earl of Burford.

## 'Wool' church

Northleach has one of the finest wool churches in the Cotswolds. Its collection of brasses are almost exclusively of the wool merchants who financed the church's construction.

## COTSWOLD FUN AND GAMES

Every Whitsun Cooper's Hill near Birdlip sees the Great Cheese Rolling Race when competitors hurtle down a forty-five degree slope in pursuit of a seven-pound cheese. Few catch it, many become walking wounded. Cheese rolling is one of many ancient sporting events in the region. The most notable is the annual Cotswold 'Olympicks' at Dover's Hill near Chipping Campden, held on the first Friday after Whitsun and dating back nearly 400 years. To rival this, Tetbury hosts the Woolsack races up the 1:4 gradient of Gumstool Hill each year on the Spring Bank Holiday. During this race a forty-eight pound sack of wool is carried in relay from the Royal Oak up to the Crown.

*Scuttlebrook Wake, Dover's Hill*

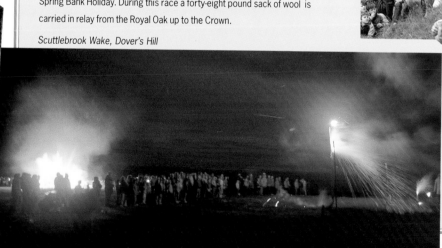

### Cider with Rosie country

This woodland path near Slad must have been one of the many explored by the young Laurie Lee during his childhood. Born in 1914, the eleventh of twelve children, Lee wrote poems of great simplicity: 'I remember, I remember the house where I was born, the little window where the sun came peeping in at dawn. He never came a wink too soon, nor brought too long a day . . .' Lee only went to the village school yet his bright imagery and deft rhythm stand alongside the more sophisticated verse of Auden, Eliot and Spender.

### Positively medieval!

Whilst many of Painswick's buildings date back to the seventeenth century, the half-timbered post office is considerably older.

### Charming prospect

This view of Painswick from Highridge near Slad is one of the best in the Cotswolds.

### Prosperous Painswick

A group of Flemish weavers came to live in the town in the sixteenth century, making it a major centre of the cloth trade for nearly 300 years. Wool dominated Cotswold life – even the name 'Cotswold' is said to originate from the Anglo-Saxon 'cote', a sheep pen, and 'wold', high uncultivated ground.

# PAINSWICK AND THE POET
## CENTRAL COTSWOLD VILLAGES

Almost half way down the Cotswold Way, just north of Stroud, lies Painswick, an impeccable little town with a large number of seventeenth- and eighteenth-century houses and a church unusually set in a churchyard crammed with ornate tombstones and tall topiary. Around Painswick lies Laurie Lee's *Cider with Rosie* country, a magical landscape that can be explored by taking the minor road south from Birdlip towards Sheepscombe and on through Jack's Green, Cockshoot and Bull's Cross to the poet's beloved Slad.

The central Cotswolds contain a number of traditional, unspoilt villages in the fine rolling countryside stretching between Painswick and Cirencester, a dozen or so miles to the east. There is Sapperton, where the poet John Masefield once lived, Bisley with its early nineteenth-century two-cell prison, and the estate village of Miserden.

**The world of Laurie Lee**

His nostalgic autobiographical novel published in 1959 recalls idyllic childhood days in the Cotswolds at the end of the First World War. The valley running down from Birdlip through Slad towards Stroud remains in a romantic timewarp.

**A tall story**

Winters can be quite harsh in the Cotswolds. Colin Brooks, for many years the head gardener at Misarden Park, can remember snow up to the top of the telegraph poles. Perhaps this is why his cottage chimney (*shown here*) is so tall!

### Entrance to a garden of delights

A steep flight of steps leads down to Painswick's main garden, entered by a wrought iron gate set in a high brick wall. The Rococo garden is the only one of its kind in the country, and never fails to delight its many visitors.

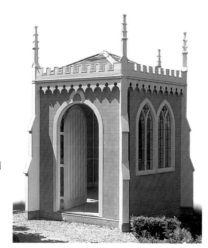

### Eagle House

This exotic construction at Painswick has been skilfully restored using an original eighteenth-century painting by Thomas Robins depicting both the Eagle House and the garden as a whole. The term 'Rococo' has been applied to garden design of the mid-eighteenth century, a period of change between the hitherto highly formal garden and the more natural look popularised by 'Capability' Brown. Rococo alluded to both symmetrical shape and flamboyant effect.

# GARDEN VARIETIES
## GREAT GARDENS OF THE CENTRAL COTSWOLDS

Just outside Painswick, the Cotswold Way passes Painswick House, noted for its highly unusual Rococo garden, which is being lovingly restored with the help of a painting of 1748. There are a number of other exquisitely varied gardens in this highly fertile part of the Cotswolds which are open to the public, including Misarden Park, Owlpen Manor and Barnsley House.

### Owlpen Manor

Just south of Stroud, Owlpen Manor is a fine Tudor manor house standing in a half-acre garden divided into five terraces. It is in a remote valley but is well worth finding.

### Scarecrow on guard

Guarded by a splendid scarecrow, Painswick's kitchen garden contains a variety of vegetables used in the eighteenth century and is bordered with fruit trees trained as espaliers. 'Feel free to walk around the garden', proclaims a notice, 'but please close the gate, we have very hungry rabbits'.

## Misarden Park

Just east of Painswick with splendid views of the Golden Valley is Misarden Park, an Elizabethan house with additions by Sir Edwin Lutyens, who also influenced the garden design, particularly the topiary and garden furniture.

## Lily pond and temple

The four-acre garden at Barnsley House, just north of Cirencester, has been lovingly developed by Rosemary Verey since 1951 and contains many rare shrubs.

## Barnsley House

This William and Mary residence complements a garden of exquisite colours and textures.

# SONG OF THE SOUTHWOLD
## INTO THE SOUTH COTSWOLDS

At Wotton-under-Edge, the Cotswold Way enters an understated, almost secret part of the Cotswolds. Narrow lanes wriggle stealthily southward through beech woods and high banks towards Hen's Edge, Bagwash and Ozleworth Bottom. The minor road from Ozleworth to Wotton-under-Edge journeys down a remote and secluded valley of great beauty. Low-profile villages such as Sherston and Easton Grey nestle half-hidden in the Avon valley, whilst the softer countryside around Tetbury is the land of the horse, where many people ride and the best compete in the great three-day equestrian events at Gatcombe Park and Badminton.

Sheep in pasture, Ozleworth Bottom

### An occupied castle

Beverston contains one of the very few surviving medieval castles, privately owned and still inhabited. Opposite is a fine Norman church with a beautifully carved Anglo-Saxon sculpture on the south face of the tower. Most of the cottages in the village have colourful, well-kept gardens.

### Horton Court

Reputedly the oldest inhabited house in England, the Cotswold Way passes this Tudor manor house just north of Chipping Sodbury. Horton Court was built around 1520 for Dr William Knight, a high flyer in the court of Henry VIII. Henry despatched him to Rome in 1527 to negotiate the king's divorce from Catherine of Aragon. The Renaissance loggia in the garden was inspired by this trip.

### A six-sided tower

The hexagonal tower of St Nicholas at Ozleworth Bottom is extremely rare, as indeed is much of the architecture in a church which dates back to the Norman Conquest. Nearby are two fine country houses, Ozleworth Park and Newark Park.

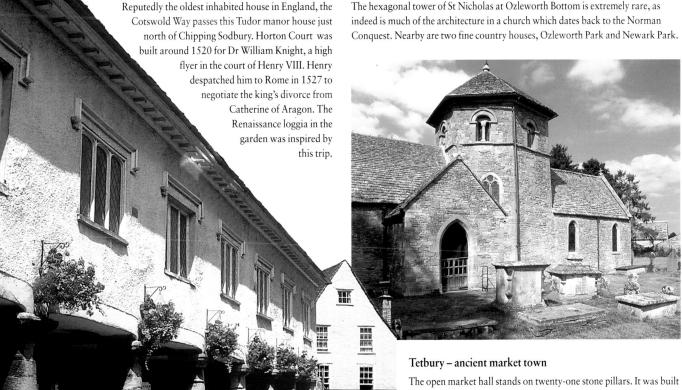

### Tetbury – ancient market town

The open market hall stands on twenty-one stone pillars. It was built in the seventeenth century but the market place originated some 400 years earlier. St Mary's church spire can be seen for miles around; less obvious but well worth seeking out is the terraced row of cottages running down the medieval cobbled steps beyond the Chipping, a small square behind the Snooty Fox whose first floor ballroom is the scene of many lively hunt balls. Tetbury is an excellent hunting ground for antiques.

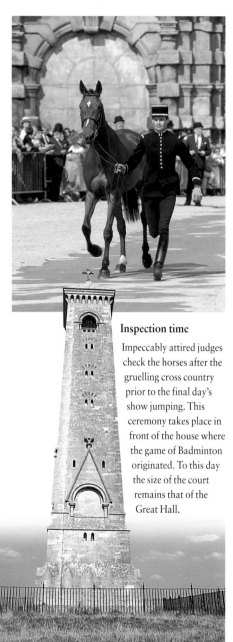

### Inspection time

Impeccably attired judges check the horses after the gruelling cross country prior to the final day's show jumping. This ceremony takes place in front of the house where the game of Badminton originated. To this day the size of the court remains that of the Great Hall.

### Splashdown!

Badminton House *(right)* lies close to the Cotswold Way, the home of the Duke of Beaufort and annual venue for the most famous three-day equestrian event in the world, consisting of dressage, cross country and show jumping. The fences on the cross country are exceedingly difficult, none more so than the water jump into the lake. The course covers nearly four-and-a-half miles through the park and attracts the largest single-day crowd of any sporting event in Britain.

### The Tyndale Monument

This tall memorial erected in 1866 stands high on the ridge above North Nibley, a small village near Wotton-under-Edge said to be the birthplace of John Tyndale. It was Tyndale who translated the Bible into English and was burnt at the stake for heresy in 1536. Two years later, Henry VIII decreed that every church in England should have an English Bible.

### Georgian manor house

This elegant country house is one of many to be found in the small village of Easton Grey.

### A well-kept secret

Down a little side lane just north of Sherston lies the delightful hamlet of Easton Grey through which flows the River Avon, one of the few rivers in the Cotswolds, crossed here by a fine arched bridge. There is a delightful river walk along the banks of the Avon from Easton Grey to Sherston.

### Autumn at Westonbirt

At this time of year the trees in the southern Cotswolds display all the vibrant colour of New England in the Fall, especially at Westonbirt Arboretum. Robert Holford started planting here in 1829, and the arboretum, which contains 18,000 trees and seventeen miles of pathways, is now run by the Forestry Commission.

### Local hero

Near the famous arboretum at Westonbirt is Sherston, an unspoilt, unheralded, unsung gem of a village. Known as 'White Walls' in Saxon, and valued at four pounds in the Domesday Book, it is perhaps best known for its association with the legend of John Rattlebones, who is said to have helped defeat the Danes in the Battle of Sherston in 1016. The fine-looking Church of the Holy Cross opposite the Rattlebone Inn has an effigy, supposedly that of the intrepid warlord.

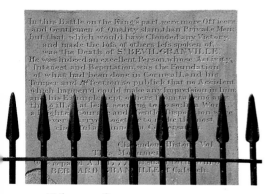

**Tribute to a fine man**

The inscription on the Lansdown Monument *(see below)* erected by Lord Lansdown in 1720 records Sir Bevil's admirable character and bravery.

**Market Square, Stow-on-the-Wold**

This historic square was the scene of battle during the Civil War when the Royalist armies under Prince Rupert were defeated as they tried to check the Parliamentarian advance on Gloucester.

# Battle Sights

## THE COTSWOLDS AS A WAR ZONE

Throughout most of the nation's turbulent history the Cotswolds managed to remain firmly beneath the parapet. During the Civil War the region was brought very much into the firing line, caught between the predominantly Royalist West Country and Wales to the west and Cromwell's Parliamentarian forces to the east. Some of the Royalists' most notable victories were gained in this area, notably Edgehill in 1642 and Lansdown in 1643. Today many traces of this tragic conflict can still be seen throughout the Cotswold countryside.

**The Lansdown Monument**

An imposing monument commemorates the battle of 5 July 1643, between King Charles's western army and the Parliamentarian forces defending Bath. The Royalist Sir Bevil Grenville led his Cornish foot soldiers up the hill to storm the enemy guns, but at the moment of victory, Sir Bevil was struck down from his horse and mortally wounded.

## A POST-WAR GHOST STORY

Colonel Nathaniel Stephens, owner of Chavenage House near Tetbury, had been an avid supporter of the Parliamentarian cause. After the war Cromwell visited Chavenage and persuaded him to add his signature to the king's death warrant. Soon afterwards the colonel was taken mysteriously ill. He left his sickbed to enter a coach driven by a headless man dressed in royal robes. The coach drove off in flames and the colonel was never seen again.

### Cotswold castles under siege

Sudeley Castle paid the price for being the king's battle headquarters and was badly damaged. It is said that another besieged castle in the village of Beverston near Tetbury was only taken after the Royalist commander had slipped out to visit his mistress and was captured with the castle keys!

### Close encounters

The Sealed Knot annually stages a number of battles in different parts of the country, as far as possible on the exact site of the original conflict. These are very dramatic and highly authentic, and over the years the society has raised more than a million pounds for charity.

**Contrasting buildings**

The variation of half-timbered buildings and traditional
Cotswold stone is a pleasing feature of Castle Combe.

**Colourful hanging baskets**

The flowers contrast with the silvery grey
Cotswold stone buildings of Castle Combe.

**Classic view**

The best approach to
Castle Combe in
Wiltshire is from the
A420 turning off at
Ford. A narrow lane
descends through thick
woods, the trees
meeting overhead
creating a dark green
tunnel, which then
emerges on to an
ancient three-arched
bridge with the village
stretching out on the far
bank. In winter the
stream is swift-flowing,
while in summer the
buildings are reflected in
calmer waters.

**Avon, still Cotswold country**

The countryside south of the motorway is still very much the
Cotswolds, with drystone walls and panoramic views south
where the Cotswold Way continues towards Bath.

# REMAINS OF THE WAY

## SOUTH COTSWOLD HOUSES AND VILLAGES

Not many people would consider the area south of the M4 which runs
towards Bath to be part of the Cotswolds, yet it is still a limestone
landscape, with fine countryside and sweeping views. Visitors will
discover an imposing baroque mansion at Dyrham Park, and Castle
Combe must be a serious contender for the title of definitive Cotswold
village. The area also contains an equally fine period house at Corsham
and a beautifully sited Elizabethan manor at Cold Ashton.

Dyrham takes its name from the Anglo-Saxon 'doer-hamm', meaning
deer enclosure, and there is still a large herd in the park. A big battle was
fought here in AD 577, when the invading Saxons captured the Cotswolds
and killed three British kings. Fortunately that was a very long time ago,
for today the area is mainly peaceful farmland.

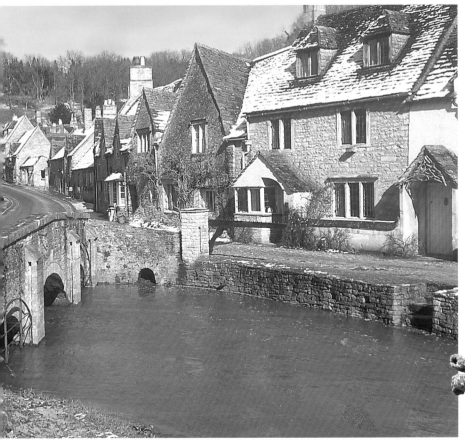

### Idyllic cottages

The weavers who lived in these cottages in Castle Combe during the Middle Ages would have had a lifestyle that was far from idyllic, working twelve hours a day for pitifully low wages.

### High up on the hill

An enormous statue of Neptune points dramatically to the house at Dyrham Park. Sadly, this statue is all that remains of a once-extensive water garden.

### Development of Dyrham Park

Dyrham Park was once the home of the Secretary of State to William III. Between 1692 and 1704 William Blathwayt employed two architects to redevelop the Elizabethan manor house. The eastern front was designed by William Talman, autocratic assistant to Sir Christopher Wren and wealthy squire, who had taken up architecture more as a hobby than as a profession.

**The Abbey today**

The third to be built on the same site, the present Bath Abbey was begun in the fifteenth century by Bishop Oliver King, who had a dream of angels climbing ladders to heaven. The interior is Perpendicular in style with later additions by Sir Gilbert Scott. The fan vaulting is particularly impressive.

**Across the bridge**

Lined with shops, Robert Adam's Pulteney Bridge gracefully spans the Avon, echoing Florence's Ponte Vecchio. Nearby is the city's major contemporary centre of excellence, the Recreation Ground, home to one of England's finest rugby teams.

# BATH – 'THE PRETTIEST CITY IN THE KINGDOM'

So Samuel Pepys acclaimed the fair city of Bath in 1668. The best was yet to come – during the next century the combined talents of three men transformed a somewhat sleazy gambling town into the chic tourist resort it is today. Energetic entrepreneur Richard Allen provided the finance, engaging John Wood, an ambitious young architect, to make the city into one of Europe's architectural showpieces, whilst the charismatic Beau Nash established the social airs and graces. Collectively they provided an irresistible formula for success. The rich and famous, and those aspiring to be, flocked to Bath making it the centre of England's smart society.

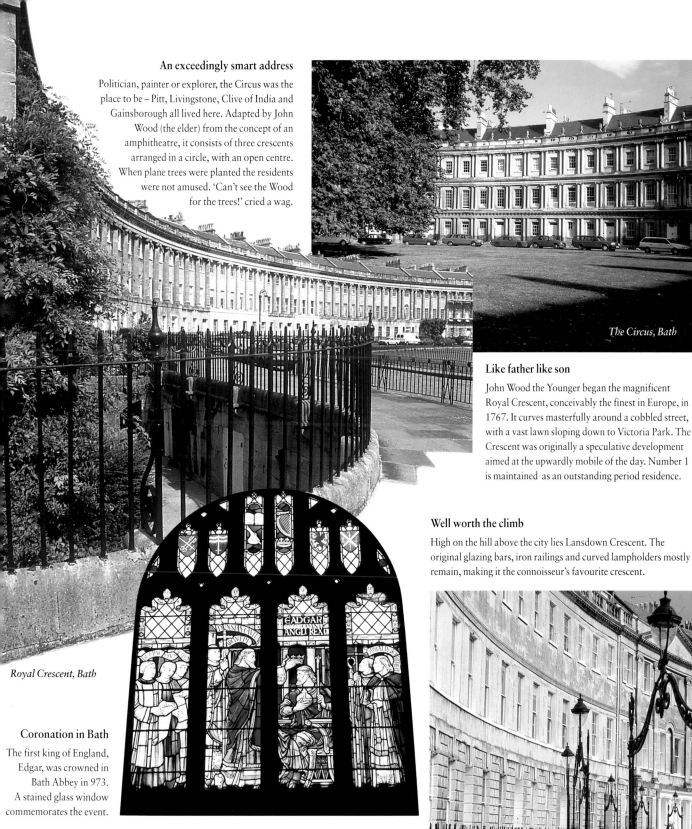

### An exceedingly smart address

Politician, painter or explorer, the Circus was the place to be – Pitt, Livingstone, Clive of India and Gainsborough all lived here. Adapted by John Wood (the elder) from the concept of an amphitheatre, it consists of three crescents arranged in a circle, with an open centre. When plane trees were planted the residents were not amused. 'Can't see the Wood for the trees!' cried a wag.

*The Circus, Bath*

### Like father like son

John Wood the Younger began the magnificent Royal Crescent, conceivably the finest in Europe, in 1767. It curves masterfully around a cobbled street, with a vast lawn sloping down to Victoria Park. The Crescent was originally a speculative development aimed at the upwardly mobile of the day. Number 1 is maintained as an outstanding period residence.

*Royal Crescent, Bath*

### Well worth the climb

High on the hill above the city lies Lansdown Crescent. The original glazing bars, iron railings and curved lampholders mostly remain, making it the connoisseur's favourite crescent.

### Coronation in Bath

The first king of England, Edgar, was crowned in Bath Abbey in 973. A stained glass window commemorates the event.

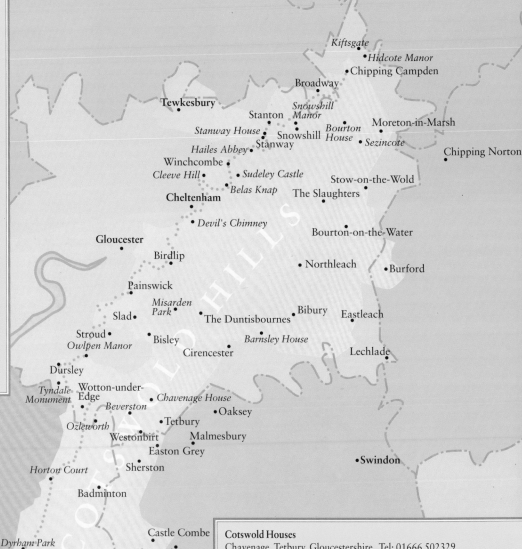

Map labels:

**Stratford-upon-Avon**
*Kiftsgate*
*Hidcote Manor*
Chipping Campden
Broadway
*Snowshill Manor*
Moreton-in-Marsh
**Tewkesbury**
Stanton
*Stanway House*
Snowshill
*Bourton House*
*Sezincote*
Chipping Norton
*Hailes Abbey*
Stanway
Winchcombe
Cleeve Hill
*Sudeley Castle*
Stow-on-the-Wold
*Belas Knap*
The Slaughters
**Cheltenham**
*Devil's Chimney*
Bourton-on-the-Water
**Gloucester**
Birdlip
Northleach
Burford
Painswick
*Misarden Park*
Bibury
Eastleach
Slad
The Duntisbournes
Stroud
*Barnsley House*
*Owlpen Manor*
Bisley
Lechlade
Dursley
Cirencester
*Tyndale Monument*
Wotton-under-Edge
*Chavenage House*
*Beverston*
Oaksey
*Ozleworth*
Tetbury
Westonbirt
Malmesbury
Easton Grey
**Swindon**
*Horton Court*
Sherston
Badminton
**Bristol**
Castle Combe
*Dyrham Park*
Chippenham
**Bath**
COTSWOLD HILLS

...... The Cotswold Way